How to

Create a Video Biography

A Legacy for Your Family

by

Ira Heffler

&

Jerry Schneider

Arrowhead Publishing
Lake Arrowhead, California

Library of Congress Catalog Card Number
Heffler, Ira and Schneider, Jerry
how to create a video biography – a legacy for your family / Ira Heffler
and Jerry Schneider
ISBN 0-9648563-7-9

1st Printing – June 1999

Publisher's Cataloging in Publication
(Provided by Quality Books, Inc.)

Heffler, Ira.
    How to create a video biography ; a legacy for
your family / by Ira Heffler & Jerry Schneider. –
1st ed.
    p. cm.
    ISBN: 0-9648563-7-9

    1.   Oral biography. 2. Interviewing in
Genealogy. 3. Video recordings— Production and
Direction. I. Schneider, Jerry (Jerry W.) II.
Title.

CT22.H44 1999   920'.0028
                                 QBI99-542

Attention Corporations and Professional Organizations:
Quantity discounts are available on bulk purchases of this book.

Table of Contents

Chapter 1

Why Create
a Video Biography?

At one time or another, each and every one of us has looked at a photograph of a grandparent or great-grandparent and wondered what that person was like. In the future, our grandchildren and great-grandchildren will wonder the same thing about us.

It has been suggested that in fifty years no one will know who we were. That no one will know we were even here – especially if we're grandparents today.

Create a Video Biography

The video biography offers a means to maintain that connection with our past and our children's past.

A video biography is so much more revealing than a diary, a scrapbook, or a photo album. More than cold statistics listing place and date of birth, it's an incredible means to reveal how someone looked, the way someone smiled, all laced with a warm glow of truth. It's a family tree that is truly alive.

When your child asks, "Mommy, what was Grandma like?" – you will not have to tell the story. You'll be able to show the "live" grandma to the child in the form of the Video Biography – *Told by the very person who lived it.*

All too often we lose touch with what really matters. We tend to get so caught up with the "now," with the acquiring of things, and with our daily routines, that we often lose sight of our past. We lose sight of our origins.

By losing that touch with our parents and our grandparents, we lose touch with our personal history. We risk losing touch with our children and their children. We lose touch with ourselves.

Use the thought-provoking questions in the script. They will help you draw out the chronicles of one's life – the highs and the lows – as well as the philosophical taking stock of a lifetime.

The interview becomes both a reflection as well as an introspection. The questions also allow the viewer to learn about the era. The telling of how ice was delivered by horse and wagon, etc., truly makes history come alive!

The interview, technical tips, and script of questions will form a richly textured profile of your Subject. You will observe first-hand your precious family history – the stories, philosophical thoughts, those "unintentionally" kept family secrets.

We are the first generation to have the technology necessary to see and hear one's life story. The technology that will share the chronicles of one's life – the stories, the anecdotes, the era, the pulling back, and taking stock of a lifetime – with one's great-great grandchildren.

There are **two** scripts included: a) one for the adult interview; and b) the youngster interview.

This manual will give you the tools and teach you the means to create an inexpensive family treasure, a legacy that will be cherished and passed down from generation to generation. It gives you the means to expose your children to a fascinating and important piece of history – their own. Pass down your loved ones and yourself – for generations to come.

Chapter 2

Creating your own video biography can be easily accomplished and a lot of fun. To do it yourself, all you need is this book, some basic equipment, and a partner.

You may already own a VCR and a video camera. If you don't have a camera, perhaps you can borrow one. They are also available for rent. Obviously, you'll also need cassettes of video tape.

You don't need sophisticated equipment. Fine results can be achieved with a modestly priced camcorder. It's best to use what you're familiar with – what you already understand.

Other equipment required or optional is shown in the Equipment List later in the book.

The video taping works best with a partner. One person functions as the **Camera Operator.** He (she) will line up the shots, help arrange the setting, lights, etc. Some experience with using a camcorder is helpful, but not necessary. A sense of color, light, and framing is a plus.

The other person is referred to in this manual as the **Moderator.** He (she) will use the script and ask questions of the Subject to guide the interview. The Moderator needs the ability to listen, as well as speak clearly, since their voice will be heard on the tape asking questions of the Subject. Making eye contact and generating a certain warmth with the Subject is important. The person whose biography you'll be taping is referred to as the **Subject** in all sections of this manual.

Create a Video Biography

Chapter 3

BASIC EQUIPMENT

Most likely you either currently own or will be able to secure the equipment and supplies necessary to produce a video biography.

This chapter deals with production equipment only. Using the equipment effectively is covered in the chapters, "Achieving Good Audio" and "Achieving Good Video." The equipment needed for a taping session includes:

- Video camera (with earphones, audio/video "out" cables, and spare camcorder batteries)
- Video tape (Keep a spare handy)
- Tripod
- Lapel microphones (lavaliere type) and a "Y" connector
- Spare microphone batteries
- Lights (2) and spare bulbs (Table lamps okay)
- Optionally, two table lamps, two light stands and clamps
- Diffusion material (white rip stop nylon) with clothes pins.
- Audio extension cables
- Electrical extension cords
- "Do Not Disturb" sign(s)
- Production check list
- Two folding chairs (optional)
- Portable color TV monitor (optional)
- Copy stand or easel to hold old photos (optional)
- This book, pen and note pad

If you do choose to use the lapel microphones, then you may utilize an omni-directional microphone. (The lapel microphones are recommended)

Although it's reasonable to suggest that more sophisticated and "high end" equipment would be best, with today's technology virtually any video camera can produce the desired results without additional lights or microphones.

VHS is the most common format and offers a consistent image quality. The 8mm format gives a very sharp image, and the cassettes are compact. Virtually any format (analog or digital) is fine. Use the camera with which you are most comfortable. Any system will work.

Important: A tripod is crucial! Don't even think of conducting a taping session with a handheld camera. Not only will you get tired of standing in one position for one and a half hours, images will be unprofessional, jiggly, and sloppy.

If you don't have a tripod then buy one, borrow one, or rent one. Photo tripods are reasonably priced. A good one may be purchased for under fifty dollars. Virtually all video cameras have a "universal thread," so camera and tripod can be attached.

Important: Although use of the camera's built-in microphone will offer fairly acceptable results, much better sound quality can be achieved by using external microphones. Most video cameras have input(s) for external microphones. The best results are achieved by using two lapel microphones, one clipped to the Subject and one clipped to the Moderator. An alternative is to use one omni-directional microphone on a stand between the Subject and the Moderator. Please refer to the chapter, "Achieving Good Audio."

Important: Although video cameras have the ability

to record under low lighting conditions, it is best to employ at least two lights and two stands and/or clamps for additional illumination. These can be ordinary table lamps. The available room light may be sufficient, but additional lights will be helpful to fill in shadows on the Subject's face with light, to light the background, and reduce video picture "noise."

Avoid the pitfall of over-lighting and flooding your Subject.
(See the Chapter "Achieving Good Video")

The two folding chairs are certainly not mandatory, but they will help with the overall look of the taping session.

A small color TV monitor will be extremely useful to preview/review image content and color control. It is more accurate than the camera viewer and gives a more accurate display. By using a monitor, the

Camera Operator may run a brief pre-roll and examine a small piece of video footage to assure a good recording. (See "The Taping Process")

A copy stand with an attached light bar helps to shoot old photographs which be edited and inserted into the final copy. If the you have a copy stand, great! If not, you can be improvise!

Bring at least two blank video cassettes to the session. We recommend you use 90 minute stock to avoid having to switch tapes during the session. Anything longer may cause extra wear and tear on the camera and tape deck. Avoid tapes that run 20 minutes or less.

The use of other equipment, such as diffusion material for lighting, is covered in the Chapter on "Achieving Good Video."

Chapter 4

ACHIEVING GOOD AUDIO

The single most important element in achieving good sound quality is to use external microphones. Use either two lapel (lavaliere type) or one central omni-directional microphone.

The lapel microphones work best. One for the Subject and one for the Moderator. These units are inexpensive and can be purchased at many electronic stores, e.g. *Radio Shack*. The mini-lapel microphones will *significantly* improve the sound quality.

Although the camera's built-in microphone may produce satisfactory results, the sound quality can be hollow or "tinny." Also, the built-in units tend to pick up more ambient room noise.

▶ Wireless microphones are expensive and unnecessary.

▶ Clip a microphone to the shirt, blouse, or dress of both Subject and Moderator. Place the microphone near the person's upper chest. Position it slightly off to one side to eliminate any explosive voice "pops."

▶ The microphones needn't be hidden. It is fine if they're visible. However, place the wire inside the Subject's shirt, blouse or dress. The wire can exit at waist level, where it won't be noticed on the tape.

▶ The Camera Operator needn't be concerned with the Moderator's microphone wire, since that person is only seen from the back.

▶ Use a "Y" connector if there's only one external microphone input (monaural) on your camcorder.

▶ Prior to actual taping, position the Subject and Moderator in their respective chairs then run a sound check. Use the earphones (plugged into the camera output) to check the volume level for "hum" or other transient line noise.

▶ Be sure to check the sound of the Moderator's microphone as well as your Subject's. Also, it's important to play the sound check back if using a TV monitor.

► Got a loud, scratchy noise? It's probably a microphone rubbing against someone's clothing. Check both the Subject and Moderator.

► If you're using either the lapel or an omni-directional microphone, the Subject and Moderator should both have impressive, full sound. This is easily verified with the pre-taping session sound check.

By following these procedures, you should achieve excellent sound quality.

Chapter 5

ACHIEVING GOOD VIDEO

With a basic sense of aesthetics, some common sense, and by following these tips, the picture quality can be quite impressive.

▶ Lighting the scene is the single most important element for the overall "look" of the video biography.

▶ Don't fall into the trap of getting carried away

with excessive lighting. Video camcorders are extremely light sensitive. In many cases, window or ambient light will be sufficient. Gone are the days when 8 mm home movies on film had that huge light bar, and everyone was bathed in light, squinting into the camera.

▶ Use an extra light source as a filler to remove unwanted shadows from your Subject's face, and as a means to illuminate the background of your Subject's home. This can be achieved by using a table lamp with the shade removed and some diffusion material. A home light fixture set-up, using two table lamps, would look like the sketch on the next page. (Figure 1-1) This is an example of two- point lighting

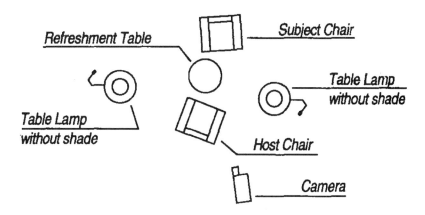

Fig. 1-1

▶ Another option is to use a professional video
   light (these video lights can be rented, but it's
   questionable economics for you to do so). If you
   do, place the video light on a stand or attach it
   with a clamp to a chair or door. See Fig. 1-2
   on the following page. Notice how the lights
   form a triangle. This is described as three-point
   lighting.

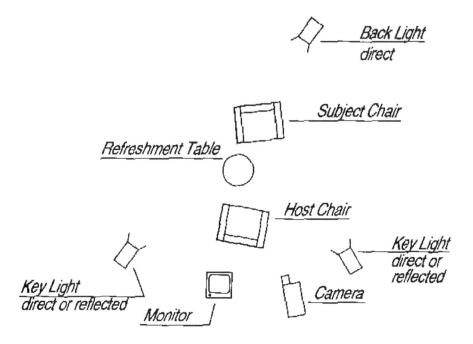

Fig. 1-2

▶ Either two or three point lighting will be fine.
Avoid mixing light sources [using a table lamp(s)]
and a "key" light, as the color of the image may
shift. Use either daylight or incandescent light,
but do not use the two sources together.

▶ "Barn doors" or shutters attached to the professional lights may be used to direct light onto a specific area. Remember to keep it soft. Diffuse the light: Use reflectors (umbrellas) or bounce the light off a white ceiling. *Avoid the common trap of over-lighting.*

▶ Another way to soften the light on your Subject is by use of a non-flammable diffusion material such as spun nylon or white rip stop nylon. Clip it loosely to the reflectors or "barn doors," allowing the air to circulate and the heat to escape. You may diffuse one or more light sources.

CAUTION: Always use flame retardant material. If in doubt about the diffusing material being flame retardant, don't use it!

▶ Remember, if a copy is made of your final tape, the contrast level will be higher than the original. Harsh lighting means greater contrast. A little fill-in light will go a long way. **Less is better.**

▶ Experiment. Do some test runs. Look at the image on the color monitor. Practice. It's the best way to learn and improve your technique.

▶ Always do a white balance color correction (if the camera warrants it). Make use of the monitor. Proper white balance renders the correct color of the scene. (See your camera manual for details concerning white balance.)

▶ **ALWAYS use a tripod.** Don't even think of doing a hand held taping session. Keep the camera stationary. Panning should be kept to a minimum.

▶ Your Subject should <u>not</u> wear stripes, "busy"

patterns, or colors that "bleed" (avoid red, white and black).

▶ Aim for a full-face image. Avoid profile and 3/4 face positioning. Place the camera over the shoulder of the Moderator and position the Subject to face the camera.

▶ Use the manual focus. Avoid the auto focus. Zoom in tight, focus, then pull *slowly* out.

▶ Proper framing is important. The steps below will guarantee good composition:

1. Divide the view screen into imaginary thirds.

2. For **wide** shots, keep the <u>face</u> in the <u>upper 2/3 right</u> or left portion of the screen. (See Figure A).

3. For a **close up**, keep the <u>eyes</u> at the line in the

<u>**upper 1/3 right**</u> or left portion of the screen. (See Figure B)

Fig. A   Fig. B

▶ Practice your zoom. The Camera Operator must

a) pan up slightly while

b) zooming in for a close-up.

Practice these two movements simultaneously. Keep it smooth. Keep the movement **slow**.

▶ Don't over-do the zoom. Granted, the zoom is fun, but if over-used it will become a gimmick and lose its effectiveness. <u>Don't create a</u>

distraction.

▶ **Tip**: A few times during the taping session, *slowly* zoom out to reveal the back of the Moderator's head, keep the shot for 30 seconds or so, then *slowly* zoom in to the Subject. Don't over do this technique but it cuts down the monotony of a "one-camera" production. Again, **less is better.**

▶ Keep the cuts to a minimum. The Camera Operator really doesn't need to cut to a shot showing the Moderator's face. The Moderator is not the star – the Subject is the star.

▶ Do not zoom in too close. An extreme close up may needlessly show wrinkles or blemishes. Help your Subject look as good as possible.

▶ The Subject should be seated in a folding or kitchen chair, sitting up as straight as possible. It helps keep the Subject from slouching. Casual is fine, but avoid slouching. It's undignified. Soft chairs may allow your Subject to slouch or slump.

Follow these suggestions. Use basic framing aesthetics plus some common sense. These elements will enable the Camera Operator to achieve impressive picture quality.

Chapter 6

▶ Allow a minimum of three hours for your session.

▶ Try to eliminate and anticipate possible disruptions – especially noisy ones.

▶ No friends, visitors, guests, or relatives. (Well, maybe one, but certainly not a group.) Please be slightly rude to any drop-in company. Put a sign on your door asking people to not ring the bell.

▶ If possible, try to have a family member or friend be prepared to greet visitors at the door – especially children. An untimely interruption could mar a good taping session.

▶ Arrange for pets to be kept away from the session.

▶ Children are always curious, but they can be disruptive to the session. You should consider making arrangements for them to be elsewhere.

▶ Disconnect all your telephones, and unplug appliances and devices that might make a noisy distraction.

What to wear:

▶ Solid colors are preferred. Do not wear red,

white, or black clothing.

▶ Avoid "busy" patterns such as "zebra" stripes.

▶ A shirt, dress, or blouse is preferable, because this facilitates microphone placement.

▶ Dress casually. Informality helps the Subject be more at ease. (Men: get a close shave to eliminate any "five o'clock shadow.")

▶ The interview should be a free-flowing conversation. Don't be concerned with achieving a flawless, polished presentation. This is not a performance. Be at ease. It won't hurt the interview if the Subject stumbles a bit – even if complete with pauses and hesitation. It's all part of a true-life biography.

Create a Video Biography

Chapter 7

PUTTING THE SUBJECT AT EASE

Stage fright. It's real. The entire interview process may provoke anxiety in some individuals. Especially those who may be shy or have little experience in public speaking. The Moderator needs to be sensitive to this reaction. Some people will relish the opportunity to talk about themselves. Others will be extremely uneasy with the process.

There are some techniques that will help make your Subject feel more comfortable and put him or her at ease. The Moderator and Camera Operator should greet their Subject warmly before setting up any equipment

Next, there should be a discussion with your Subject as to which room would be best suited for the interview. Allowing your Subject to be included in much of the decision making process makes the individual feel more involved, and helps to put the Subject at ease.

Before seating your Subject review the selection of still photographs (if any) to be included.

Once in position, but before the taping begins, the Moderator (and/or the Camera Operator) should explain what to expect and the dynamics involved.

Talk to your Subject. Explain how the script consists of two areas that will be covered:
1. A chronological journey through a lifetime
2. A taking stock of the notable events in one's life

Ask your Subject if he or she has anything to share. Do this "on camera." It may be a painting, a piece of ceramic, pottery, or a coin collection. These will be referred to as "inserts."

Showing "insert aids" during the interview can be quite effective. It's insightful, adds texture, and often helps lower the anxiety of the Subject.

The Moderator must be sure to note the use of these "inserts" in the script the Subject is using.

Explain that tangents or diversions from the questions are fine. If your Subject wants to digress and expound on certain thoughts or recollections, encourage the subject to go for it!

Stress that this is an informal talk. Point out that's why your Subject is dressed casually. It's not meant to be a stiff, formal portrait.

Remind your Subject that no one is looking for a polished, flawless performance. It's okay to search for the right word. Even pausing and stumbling is fine. It's who that person is. Simply let the thoughts flow.

As the Camera Operator adjusts for light and sound, the Moderator should read aloud the Introduction from the Profile Sheet so your Subject knows what will be said at the start of the taping. Make sure your Subject approves.

▶ Briefly review what your Subject wrote in the Profile Sheet.. Your Subject should be reminded and primed on this specific information.

▶ Remind your Subject that he or she can call "cut" at any time. It probably won't happen, but it puts people at ease knowing they can do this.

▶ It helps to have a glass of water nearby for the Subject and Moderator

▶ Finally, tell your Subject to ignore the camera, and just talk to the Moderator. Ignore the lights, ignore the Camera Operator while just looking and talking only to the Moderator.

The Subject will feel more comfortable if the Moderator:

1. Uses the Subject's first name

2. Speaks with a "feeling," sympathetic tone of voice

3. Uses eye contact

4. Listens effectively and patiently

5. Controls reactions without interrupting

Employing all of these tips will help to put the subject at ease. This is important for your video to be completed as a cut above the average.

Chapter 8

THE PRE-INTERVIEW

An effective video biography hinges on a script that is tailored to the Subject. By making minor shifts, additions and deletions, there will be a stronger interplay between Moderator and Subject.

There are many significant advantages to gathering as much pre-interview information as possible about your Subject.

▶ First, it's an effective means for the Moderator to

cover important aspects that may have been overlooked. Example: Your Subject's greatest life accomplishment was helping to paint the Golden Gate Bridge. He forgot to mention it in the interview. And the Moderator neglected to bring it up. This should be included in his biography. This scenario can't happen by using the Pre-Interview Profile. The Moderator will know all the pertinent material beforehand and plug the information into the script at the appropriate places. Following this procedure will ensure that the Moderator won't make an inadvertent exclusion.

▶ Second, by incorporating the Pre-Interview Profile, the Subject will be more apt to remember specific pertinent information at the appropriate time and most likely won't even need the Moderator's gentle reminders. The process of completing the forms acts as a memory jogger.

▶ Third, with your Pre-interview Profile, the

Moderator will know in advance what the Subject did or did not do. Example: your Subject did not attend college. During the interview the Moderator might ask about college, and there's a mumbled, "I didn't go to college." This response can appear to be negative and the Subject may be a bit embarrassed. This won't happen by employing the Pre-Interview Profile.

▶ Fourth, there will be a "handle" on the person before the interview. The Moderator will know enough about the person's lifetime to allow both people to be more "together." Knowing information will affect the comfort level between the two, and a better dynamic will enhance the tone of the interview.

The Profile Sheet is used primarily for the Introduction, and as the means to obtain the Pre-interview information. We <u>strongly</u> recommend using it.

Additional Subject Profile Sheets and Script Introductions are provided as "tear outs" in the back of the book so they may be copied them for other Subjects.

The responses to some questions are "plugged" into specific script areas, with ample space on the facing "notes" page for the Moderator to write in information. Holding the profile sheets with the script and referring to them at the appropriate times may offer satisfactory results; however, we feel that writing the information on the appropriate "notes" page within the script will prove more effective for the beginning Moderator.

Responses to other questions are not designed for any particular section of the script. The Moderator will need to evaluate the information and place it in its most appropriate area.

It is not necessary for the Moderator to conduct an actual pre-interview. Have the Subject complete the information a few days in advance so the Moderator will have ample time to effectively "plug" it into the script.

The video biography cannot be all-inclusive. An entire lifetime can't be covered in less than two hours. However, the Pre-Interview profile process will help assure that specific information is not inadvertently left out of the interview.

This encompasses specific information to be included during the interview.

If there is some specific information the subject wishes to have mentioned, this is the best opportunity to do that.

You will be able to talk about these areas during the interview. List any specific information you feel is vital. This will prevent completing the interview without those elements you want included.

Perhaps more important, writing this information out now will help jog your memory of these specifics during the interview.

The interview should be spontaneous and free-flowing. You will be hearing most of the interview questions for the first time. Try and keep it on a conversational level – not a series of questions and answers.

Subject's Profile Sheet

- Date of scheduled interview _____

- City where you currently live (if different from where interview will take place)

  _____

- Your complete name (as you wish to be introduced)

  _____

- Place of birth

  _____

- Are you comfortable having the interviewer divulge your age at the beginning of the interview? _____

    a. If so, please state your date of birth _____

    b. Making you _____ years of age (at time of taping)

Create a Video Biography

- Your primary career

  ._____

- Are you currently retired? _____

- Name of current spouse (if applicable)

  _____

- Number of years married to current spouse

  _____

- Name(s) of previous spouse(s) and number of
  years married (if applicable)

  _____

- List the name(s) of your children (if applicable)
  and birth dates

  _____

  _____

  _____

With which spouse (if applicable)

- List the name(s) and age(s) of any grandchildren

and great-grandchildren (if applicable)

_____

_____

_____

_____

_____

_____

_____

Personal Data

1. Education

Did you attend high school?　　Yes　　　No

Did you attend college?　　　　Yes　　　No

2. Talents/Skills/Abilities

_____

_____

_____

_____

_____

_____

_____

3. Accomplishments/Achievements/Awards

_____

_____

_____

_____

_____

4. Honors/Scholarships

_____

_____

_____

_____

5. Did you serve in the military   Yes   No

    a. Which Branch?_____

    b. When did you serve?_____

c. Were you overseas?_____

d. Any campaigns?_____

Where?

_____

_____

_____

6. Additional careers/Jobs

_____

_____

_____

_____

_____

7. Places/Countries you've traveled

_____

_____

_____

_____

8. Hobbies/Interests

_____

_____

_____

_____

_____

_____

9. Stories/Anecdotes

_____

_____

_____

_____

_____

10. Any other specific occurrence,

experience, or event you wish to have

included? (Both the joys and heartbreaks)

_____

_____

_____

_____

_____

11. Is there a specific person or event you want to avoid mentioning?

_____

_____

_____

_____

_____

Be sure to avoid memorizing any "canned" responses from these two pre-interview profile sheets. We want to see the "wheels" turning. More important than what you say is how you say it – in your mannerisms, your style. Your personality will shine through.

Create a Video Biography

Chapter 9

BECOMING A DIRECTOR

The Video Biography Script has been tested, modified and proven. The authors have used this script in video taping hundreds of biographies. It works very well, but is flexible enough to be modified to suit the needs of the Subject.

The Moderator must review the script, then adapt it appropriately for the Subject. Eliminate the questions that aren't appropriate. Change some questions that fit what's particularly unique about your Subject. Add questions that are appropriate. Make the script comfortable to use and comfortable for the Subject's responses. After all, the Moderator is the one who has to use the script which is the tool to taping a good interview.

Know the questions. Get familiar with them. They shouldn't be memorized, but they need to be asked with feeling while maintaining eye contact with the Subject.

Although the camera will be primarily positioned over the shoulder of the Moderator, there must be effective eye contact between the Moderator and the Subject.

The Subject is the star – not the Moderator. When the Subject is speaking, the Moderator must look at the Subject rather than scan the script for the next question. Be subtle when turning pages. Make the interview more than the reading of questions. Show interest. Learn to listen and demonstrate a "controlled reaction." If the Moderator conducts the interview in this manner, he/she is subconsciously "directing" the Subject's response. It will help to put the Subject at ease

The Moderator must listen._ This isn't as easy as it sounds. For example: at the beginning of the interview, the Subject says she was an only child. Later on, if the Moderator asks if the Subject has any brothers or sisters, *even though it's in the script*, this question would be a glaring error.

The effective Moderator will use the "only child" remark as a springboard. "What was it like not having any brothers or sisters? Did you enjoy the attention or did you feel cheated?"

If your Subject is a retired pilot and has a passion for

airplanes (you'll know that in advance via the Pre-interview), it's the Moderator's responsibility to develop a series of questions that pertain to this area of interest. This will elicit strong responses. These questions should be written out on the appropriate "notes" page opposing the script questions.

For best results, use the script as a guideline, or as a catalyst for other questions. If it feels right, don't hesitate to eliminate certain questions during the interview. There is room on the opposite blank page to make notes during the interview. Follow-up questions from the Moderator's notes will help keep the interview dynamic.

The "Notes" pages have three functions:

1. To "plug in" information from the Pre-Interview profile sheets
2. To prepare additional questions <u>prior</u> to the

Interview

3. To jot down additional questions <u>during</u> the
   Interview

Avoid questions that call for one word responses.

The interview needs to have an atmosphere of
relaxation. Probe. Be persistent. But do it gently.
After all this is an interview, not an interrogation.

If the Moderator feels the interview is not working
well, move on to the next section of questions.
(Highlight those words which designate a subtle shift
in subject areas.) A certain topic may make the
Subject uncomfortable. Know when to drop
something and move on.

If the Subject volunteers something interesting, use
it as a springboard to delve deeper. This will add
more texture. Welcome the tangent. It's coming
from the Subject's heart, so it'll probably be a gem of

a recollection. However, be sure to steer the Subject back to the original question.

Allowing the questions to merge into one another will keep the interview fluid.   Let the interview evolve into a smooth, free-flowing exchange.

Do not allow the Subject to "preview" any of the questions. Sharing the questions in advance may lead to prepared responses. These kinds of responses would eliminate spontaneity and rob the viewer of what the video biography is all about.

Be sure to occasionally address the Subject by first name throughout the interview. Informality generates a feeling of familiarity and warmth. The interview process becomes more personable and helps put the Subject at ease.

Although the interplay should seem like a

conversation, there is a fine line here. It may be necessary for the Moderator to react to what is said, especially if the Subject is nervous. The Moderator need not be a cold objective interviewer with a list of questions. It's okay to react. It's okay to show surprise. It's okay to laugh. This type of response by the Moderator will help to put the Subject at ease.

However, if the Subject is "rolling along," reactions should be kept to a minimum. The Moderator should respond with eye contact and little else. With a Subject who's verbal and "open," let it be more of a monologue, and less of a conversation. After all, the Subject's great-grand children aren't viewing this to hear the Moderator's quips and comments.

Some Subjects will prove to be a "difficult" interview. The Moderator may have to work to "pull responses out" of them.

Other Subjects may "run with it" as they tell their story. The Moderator should allow the process to occur as long as the original script is returned to later. Guide the flow. This is obviously a subjective call.

Much of what the Moderator does or doesn't do depends upon the personality of the Subject. The Moderator will get better with practice as he/she conducts more interviews on other family members and friends.

Chapter *10*

The following step-by-step process for the taping session was developed by the authors, and has been refined over several hundred sessions. Obviously, you can make changes, but this basic procedure works well. The Camera Operator and Moderator must work together as a team, and if the duties are shared as below, you will achieve excellent results. Allow one hour to set up and two hours for the session.

I. BEFORE THE TAPING SESSION

➢ MODERATOR

1. Send the Subject the "Instructions for Taping Session."
2. Insert the information into the Script the Subject has provided on the "Pre-Interview" Profile
3. Compose the "Subject's Introduction."

II. DAY OF THE TAPING SESSION:

➢ MODERATOR

1. Dress appropriately – (no tank tops, etc.)
2. Complete any script revisions

➢ CAMERA OPERATOR

1. Check all the gear and review the Equipment Supply list. Remember the video tape!

III. AT THE TAPING SITE

➢ CAMERA OPERATOR

1. Select the best room for the taping
2. Set-up lights, camera, microphone, etc. (Position camera over the shoulder of Moderator)
3. Disconnect all telephones
4. Place a "Do Not Disturb" sign on the front door

➢ MODERATOR

1. Talk with the Subject about the Process (see Putting the Subject at Ease)
2. Help with equipment set up
3. Discuss session with Camera Operator

➢ CAMERA OPERATOR

1. Fine-tune lighting set up
2. Give microphones to Subject and Moderator
3. Conduct a voice and microphone check – especially for line noise
4. Zoom camera in on Subject, check focus, and zoom out to prepare the opening shot
5. "White balance" the camera. (see camera manual)
6. Run a thirty-second pre-roll
7. Be sure Subject is sitting up straight and is comfortable

➢ MODERATOR

1. Make Subject comfortable & relaxed
2. Emphasize informality
3. Remind Subject to ignore camera and

Camera Operator

4. Remind Subject it's okay bring in tangents and asides to the questions

5. Remind Subject it's okay to ask for a "break" at any time

IV. DURING THE SESSION

➤ CAMERA OPERATOR

1. Give a "countdown" and cue Moderator to start the Subject's Introduction

2. Do as much in-camera editing as possible during session

3. At conclusion of session, Camera Operator says, "Cut." Moderator and Subject to remain seated until this cue is given

4. At the end of the session, Camera

Operator may elect to tape "option enhancement" inserts e.g., old photos, Subject's hobby, etc. These will be edited and inserted into the tape later

Use 90-minute cassettes. Have at least one extra. Try to keep the interview at 90-minutes (though it may run longer).

Chapter 11

EDITING TO ENHANCE

*This chapter contains information on advanced
editing techniques, and may be a bit difficult for an
inexperienced or new camcorder owner. By
carefully reviewing this chapter, and the material
in your camcorder manual, you should be able to
achieve good results. Practice makes perfect. There
are several options which can be used for editing.*

Assemble Edit

Your Subject has a photo, a piece of artwork, or

a hand-made artifact he or she wants to include in the biography. This is commonly referred to as an *assemble* edit. To accomplish an *assemble* edit, employ the following procedures:

1. Pause Recording
2. Fill Viewing Frame with object to be filmed
3. Resume Recording (Subject to talk about object)
4. Pause recording when finished
5. Refocus on Subject
6. Continue Recording

Please refer to your camcorder manual for specific editing information applicable to your camera.

Try to utilize a small TV monitor during the edit. The larger screen will make editing much easier. Refer to your camcorder manual for proper connections.

The in-camera assemble edit may also be used to show your Subject's involvement with an activity or hobby. Use the same procedure described above to include the Subject at a different location, such as painting or gardening.

Titles

Home-made titles may be prepared and recorded prior to the interview. Create titles on 8-1/2 x 11 sheets of white or colored paper using letter colors that contrast well to the background. Make sure your titles are evenly lit. Get creative!

1. FILL the frame of the camcorder with the title to give a clean appearance on screen.
2. Some camcorders have titling capabilities that can be superimposed directly over the Subject or a color background. Refer to your camcorder's manual for this procedure.

Breaks

There are times when the Subject wishes to "break" and says so while the camera is rolling:

1. The Camera Operator should erase the request if it was recorded

2. Put the camcorder on **Playback** Mode and search for a good spot to stop or cut

3. Pause at that point and put the camera back into **Record** Mode

4. Change the **Zoom** or angle to avoid the look of a "jump" cut. This is <u>very</u> important

5. Press **Record** and cue your Subject *(by pointing)* as an indication to continue when the "break" is over

Insert Edit

The other means of editing is the "insert" edit. With this method, a different video image is inserted over the original video footage.

Caution: Once the new image is inserted over the existing video, the original taped material will have been erased. There is no way to retrieve it Therefore, you may want these inserts made on a <u>copy</u> of the original interview tape, allowing the camera master to remain unedited.

Note: You will need a TV monitor to perform an insert edit.

Important: Practice this insert edit technique on a "test" segment of tape that is not part of your interview.

Editing to Enhance

Most camcorders and VCR's have an insert edit function. There are a couple of ways to accomplish this. To use your camcorder only for inserts:

1. Choose a scene or subject you wish to insert into your existing video footage
2. Find the place in your existing video footage where you want the insert to end.
3. Reset the tape counter to "0000"
4. Rewind the tape to the point where the insert is to Begin
5. Pause
6. Focus on the subject to be inserted
7. Use the **insert function button** to add the new footage
8. Stop when you reach the "0000" point on counter

Some camcorders have a memory function that will automatically stop the insert edit at "0000." **(See the camcorder manual for details on**

insert edits.) Keep the inserts brief. Usually no more than ten seconds.

Important: The insert function will erase the Hi-Fi stereo track. Only the monaural track on the audio portion of the tape will be heard. To play the finished product, you will need to select the mono track on your VCR or make another copy of the edited tape and record the copy in stereo.

If your Subject wants to insert several old photographs, an old home movie, and a 15th century vase after you've finished the interview, don't panic. Here's the procedure:

1. Review the photos and the "home movie" video to determine the best place for the insertion. (Put a yellow "Post-it" note on the back of each photo to organize the sequence)
2. For best results the photo should be no

smaller than 3-1/2 x 5 inches.

3. Use a copy stand or affix the photos to a wall.

4. Forward the tape to provide at least a sixty second interval from the end of the interview to the beginning point of the first photo insert.

5. Better yet, you may record the section to be inserted on a separate video cassette.

6. Record each photo for approximately thirty seconds. Then record that priceless old vase and any other items to be inserted.

For the next step you will need a VCR **and** the camcorder, or two VCR's.

1. Refer to the manual concerning the insert edit functions and cable hook up on your camcorder

2. Place the original tape or camera master in either the Camcorder or the "A" VCR, and

the blank tape in the "B" machine.

3. **To be safe, mark the machines "play"
   and "record" to avoid confusion.** (You
   don't want to tape over the "master") It is
   best to break off the tab on the spine of the
   cassette of the master to avoid accidental
   erasure.

4. Make a copy of the master. *Note the
   counter number on a piece of paper
   as to where you want to insert the
   new footage.* You will need this note later
   to assemble the edits.

5. When the copy is finished, rewind the
   "record" machine to the starting point and
   find the first insert item on the "play"
   machine. At the designated spot on the
   "record" machine, insert approximately ten
   seconds of the thirty seconds previously
   recorded.

If you are using the camcorder and one VCR

for insert edits instead of two VCRs, <u>use the camera as the play deck</u>. – **not as the record deck!**

Once you have inserted all the insert material from the camera master (old photographs, objects, Subject performing a hobby or activity), remove the tape and replace it with the video tape of the old movies. Perform the same functions as outlined above.

To add titles or background music, perform the same basic steps with a tape deck or compact disc player. Refer to your VCR/camcorder manual for audio insert instructions.

Naturally, insert edits may also be used effectively to eliminate distractions, redundancy, or anything your Subject wants removed. This method also allows for a smooth transition when changing cassettes.

Other "options to enhance" may be accomplished with either the assemble or insert edit.

Examples:

• Newspaper headlines. A tight shot of the front page of that day's newspaper is taped. Either the Moderator or Subject may read the headlines of three or four current news stories. Used as a time frame, this reference makes for an effective Introduction.

• Tour of the house – the Subject escorts the Moderator and Camera Operator through the house, as framed photographs, various objects, etc., are pointed out with narration by the Subject.

• Your "life in pictures." A montage of many photographs assembled and video taped as your Subject reflects on each one. This scene could be

electronically edited with graphic titles, fades, etc.
Or, it could be a collection of in-camera "assemble"
edits. For best results, the Camera Operator would
run the tape while the Subject watches the monitor
and records her description and thoughts on each
photograph.

- Hobby Inserts. Your Subject may have described
a passion for oil painting. While the Subject is
speaking, insert a five second scene showing the
Subject at an easel. (This insert would have been
recorded <u>after</u> the interview.)

A home editing system will achieve optimum results.
Stand-alone editors or a personal computer with the
proper hardware (including sufficient memory) and
software can accomplish all of the mentioned edits.
More and more personal editing systems are
becoming available.

One product which <u>doesn't</u> require a personal computer (a stand-alone system) is :

- **"Home Video Producer "** by Videonics. Some of the features this system offers are:
     Works with virtually all camcorders and VCRs
     Stores over 200 scenes in memory
     Built-in video enhancer
     Previews sections before final assembly
     Works with all video tape formats
     Locates and records selected scenes
     Portable – can work on batteries or AC
     Sound effects mixer

  Cost: About $330 includes the editor, an easy set-up video tape, speakers and microphone.

A computer system can add high quality to your video with state of the art image-making capabilities. This software is capable of producing very sophisticated tapes.

One system that has received high praise and reviews is:

- **Avid Cinema** by Avid Technology. This software and is available for Windows 95, Windows 98, and the Macintosh.

A few of **Avid Cinema's** features are:

> Tabular interface
>
> Timeline Editing
>
> Storyboard templates for home, office & school
>
> More than two dozen special effects
>
> Title tools with arrays of fonts, animation, etc.
>
> Multiple movie formats (including VHS)

Cost: About $150 (Plus a new video card)

Check with your computer dealer on hardware requirements. For example, you must also have a

CD-ROM, a minimum of a 200 MHz Pentium II processor, an available AGP or PCI slot for a video card, and lots of available hard drive storage. (To edit a 30 minute video requires 2.1 GB)

If you are not familiar with the editing/graphics equipment, be prepared for a learning curve. With practice, you will become comfortable and proficient and soon be producing effective edits and graphics. Be patient. It will be worth the time and effort.

An alternative to your own editing is to hire a video post-production house. They have all the equipment and expertise to accomplish those effects you want. However, be prepared. They charge by the hour.

An advantage in having a professional do the work is picture quality. The normal degradation of picture quality on a second generation tape can be minimized with professional technology.

Edits, graphics, inserts of old photographs, titles, music, sound effects etc., can add a great deal of color when included in the video biography.

Chapter 12

The Taping Session

These questions are to be asked by the Moderator.
It is important to speak in a normal tone of voice. It
is even more important that you speak clearly and
distinctly without slurring your words.

Practice your questions with a simple tape recorder
before doing the interview – it will pay big dividends.

Video Biography

Script Introduction

Today is _____ _____, 19____,
             (Month)   (Day)

and we're in _____, ___ taping the
           (City)   (State)

Video Biography of :

_____
                  (Subject)

(Background information from Pre-interview Profile Sheet. Place and date of birth; career/retired(?), where living (if different from above; names of siblings - and where they live; name of current spouse- years married?; names of children; names and ages of grandchildren, etc.)

_____

_____

_____

_____

_____

_____

Questions

- Let's begin with your family background, *(Subject's first name)*

- What is your full name? (Maiden name, if applicable)

- Were you named after anyone?

- Do you have a nickname? How did the nickname come about?

- Do you have brothers or sisters, (Subject's first name)?

    Are they alive or deceased?
    What are their names and ages?
    Where do they live?

Notes:

- When did your earliest ancestors arrive in
  this country?
  > Why did they come to America?
  > Are there any stories that have been handed
  > down about them?
  > Revolutionary war? Civil War? Pioneers?
  > Ellis Island?

- Your parents...
  > What (are) were their names?
  > Where and when were they born?
  > If not born here, then where?
  > When did they immigrate?
  > Why did they come here?
  > > Religious persecution?
  > > Political?
  > > Economic?

- Did they ever tell you stories of their childhood?
  > Tell us you favorite remembered story
  > Are they still living?   When did they die?
  > What were their occupations?

Notes:

- Do you remember your grandparents?

- What are your memories of them?

      What were their names?

      Where were they born?

      Did they immigrate?

      Why did they come to this country?

      Religious persecution?

      Political?

      Economic?

- Did they ever tell you or your parents childhood stories?

         Tell us your favorite

- Are your grandparents still living?

- When did they die?

- If not in the U.S., then where?

Notes:

- Talk about your aunts and uncles

- What do you know about earlier ancestors?

- Did your ethnic origin have an influence on you?

- Do you have any famous relatives?

- Has anyone in your family achieved notoriety?

- Are there any "black sheep" in your family?
    Who are they?
    What did they do?

- Has your ethnic origin influenced your life?
    How?

- Go back to your earliest childhood memory

    How old are you?

Notes:

Where are you?

What's happening?

- Where did you live when you were a small child?

- Can you describe your house?

- Can you describe your neighborhood?

- Where did you go to elementary school?

    Was it close to your home?

    How did you get to school?

    Describe your teacher

    Describe your classroom

    Describe the playground

- Do you have any vivid memories of elementary school?

- Were you a good student?

Notes:

• How did you get along with your schoolmates?

• How did you get along with your brothers and sisters?

> Did you fight?
>
> Were you friends?
>
> Do you have any vivid memories?

• How did you spend your summers as a child?

> Did you take family vacations?
>
> Do you have photographs of those trips?
>
> Do you remember your first train or plane ride?

• Did you have any pets when you were a child?

> What were their names?

• What games did you play?

> Which was your favorite game?
>
> Who did you play with?

Notes:

- Who was your best friend?

   What was his/her name?

   Have you kept in touch?

- As a child, did you have a sense of whether your family was rich or poor?

- Did you have a favorite toy?

- Do you have a special memory of your mother?

   Of your father?

- Were you disciplined as a child?

   How?

- Were you happy as a child?

   Do you have fond memories of growing up?

Notes:

- Let's move on to high school

  What was the name of your high school?

- What city were you living in?

- Think back to a specific incident in high school

  Where are you?

  What's happening?

- Were you a good student?

  What was your favorite subject?

  What was your least favorite?

- Did you have active extra-curricular activities?

  Sports?

  Yearbook?

  Cheerleading?

  Drama Club?

  Any others?

Notes:

- Any awards, achievements, or scholarships?

- Who was your best friend?

- Are you still in contact with any high school friends?

- Who was your favorite teacher?

     What made him/her so special?

- What did you do after school?

- As a teenager . . .

     Were you outgoing or shy?

     Were you sociable or keep to yourself?

- Did you have a favorite movie?

     A favorite song?

- Did have a favorite radio or TV show?

Notes:

- Did you have a "steady?"

    Who?

      Have you kept in touch?
- Did you have a secret love?

    Who?
- Who was the first person you ever kissed?

- Did you attend your senior prom?

- Who was your date?

- What kind of dancing was popular then?

- Do you wish high school could have been different or better in any way?

- Do you remember learning to drive a car?

    How old were you?

    Who taught you?

    Describe the car

Notes:

What were the roads like?

- Were there family vacations during the summer?

  Which was your favorite one?

- What were your responsibilities around the house?

- Did you get an allowance?

  How much?

- Did the Great Depression of the '30's impact your family?

- How would you summarize your teen years?

- Did you attend college or vocational school?

  Which one(s)?

  What did you study?

  Did you belong to a fraternal organization?

  Which one?

Notes:

- What was your best talent in college?

- Did you receive any awards or scholarships?

  Were you active in sports?

  Other activities?

- Do you have any vivid memories of college?

  Describe them

  Did you graduate?

- Who was your best friend in college?

- Are you still in touch?

- Have you stayed in touch with any others?

- Who did you date in college?

- Did it turn into a romance?

Notes:

- Have you stayed in touch?

- Did you serve in the military?

- Which branch?

- Where were you stationed?

- Tell me about being in the service

- What were you doing during World War II?
    Korea?
    Viet Nam? Any others?

- How did wartime affect your life?

- When did you first leave home as an adult?

- Where did you move to?

Notes:

- Tell me about the first place you lived on your own.

- How much did you pay for rent?

- Is this where you lived during most of your adult life?

- What was your first job after you left home?

- How much did you earn?

- Did you enjoy this work?

- What eventually became your main career?

- What were your duties? What was your job description?

- What was the most frustrating part of it?

Notes:

- If you could have chosen a different career,
  what would it have been?

- Were you married during this job?

- What is/was your (first, second) husband's/wife's
  full name?
  (In order. if previous spouses.)
- When, where, and how did you meet?

  - Tell me about your first date

- On that first date, did you have any idea that this
  person might become significant in your life?

- What attracted you to this person?

- What do you suppose this person found attractive
  about you?

Notes:

- Was it love at first sight?

- What was your courtship like?

- How long from the time you first met until you got married?

- Where did you go on your honeymoon?

- After marriage, did you have any surprises?

- Do you remember your first argument as a newly wed?

  What was it about?

- Who were the other married couples you saw frequently?
- Are you still married to your first spouse?

  How many years? (or)

Notes:

- How did this marriage end?

   (Repeat this section for each spouse)

- What's the most important quality in selecting a spouse?

- Is marriage everything you expected?

- What are the names of your children?

- When were they born?

(Be sure it's clear if children were from a former spouse.)

- Where are they currently living?

- Are they married?
   To whom?

Notes:

- Think back to the day your first child was born.

  (Pause)

  Tell me about the experience

- What's the best thing about children?

- And the most frustrating?

- Can you give me a brief summary about your grandchildren

(Include names of their spouses, where they live, names and ages of children, etc.)

- What's it like to be a grandparent?

- As a grandparent, do you travel as often?

- Do you enjoy traveling?

Notes:

- Where have you traveled to?
  When? With whom?

- What is the most extraordinary trip you've taken?

- What are the most spectacular sights you've seen while traveling?

- Did you mingle with the people?
  Did you talk to them?

- What is your greatest memory from any trip?

- Where would you like to travel next?

- Other than traveling, what are your interests or hobbies?

- What do you like to do for fun?

Notes:

- What talents or abilities have you developed?

- What talents or hobbies would you like to accomplish?

- Do you speak any other language other than English?

- Have you ever played a musical instrument? Which one?

- Do you play cards?

- Do you collect or make things? Stamps, coins, antiques, models, artwork, etc.? **(If so, have samples for later taping)**

- Do you belong to any social groups or organizations?

Notes:

- What are some other favorite things in life . . .

   Your favorite food?

- Do you have a favorite recipe you'd like to

   share with your future generations?

- Are you more attracted to the city or the country?

- Favorite newspapers & magazines?

- Favorite authors?   Books?

- Do you watch TV?

- What's your favorite current TV show?

- Your favorite TV show of all time?

- Do you enjoy and go to the Movies?

   Favorite film?

Notes:

- Favorite actors/actresses?

  Favorite singers/musicians?

  Favorite comedians?

  Who makes you laugh?

  Your favorite holiday?

  Why?

- Do you like our country's way of governing?

  How patriotic are you?

- Are you a liberal or conservative?

- Are you frugal or fiscally conservative?

- Are you a Democrat or a Republican?

  Why?

- Who did you vote for in the last election?

  Why?

Notes:

- Have you ever worked in a political campaign?

  When?

  For whom?

- Do you believe war can ever be justified?

  Under what circumstances?

- How did war have an effect on your life?

- Are you passionate about social issues or causes?

(Suggest a few contemporary issues listed here.)

  The death penalty?

  Should abortions be legalized?

  Mercy killing/euthanasia?

  What about the homeless?

  Should we help the starving of the world, or help our own people first?

- Is it the government's responsibility to ensure that all of its people are healthy?

Notes:

How about Social Security ?

Medicare?

- You've witnessed many significant historical events.   What were you doing when...

  ✓ Charles Lindberg flew from New York to Paris in 1927?

  ✓ The Hindenberg exploded in 1937?

  ✓ Pearl Harbor was attacked in 1941?

  ✓ D-Day in 1942?

  ✓ President Kennedy's assassination ('63)?

  ✓ Martin Luther King and/or Bobby Kennedy's assassinations in 1967?

  ✓ The lunar landing in 1969?

  ✓ President Nixon's resignation in 1974?

  ✓ The Berlin Wall fell?

  ✓ The Soviet Union's collapse in 1991?

- Do we have too much government in our lives?

Notes:

- Is our government doing what it needs to do . . .

   Internationally ?

   Politically?

   Economically?

   Socially?

- What has been the saddest or most frustrating experience in your life?

- What has been your greatest accomplishment?

- And your greatest disappointment?

- What is the most important thing in your life right now?

- Do you feel you've had a lucky (blessed) life?

- Is there anything you would have done differently - professionally or personally?

Notes:

If so, what?

- What quality about yourself are you <u>most</u> proud of?

- What quality about yourself are you <u>least</u> proud of?

- What would you like to change about yourself?

- Any bad habits?

- What are you afraid of?

- Do you have a pet peeve?
  What really "bugs" you?

- As an adult, what are your impressions of your parents?

- Describe your disposition

Notes:

- Are you a strong or a passive person?

    Are you warm and friendly?

    Are you sometimes distant?

    Do you get moody?

- How is your health?

    How are you feeling these days?

- Do you have any more goals you'd like to accomplish?

- Can you prioritize your goals?

- If a "Genie" granted you three wishes, what would they be?

- Have there been any "life lessons" you've learned?

- What's the most important one you've learned?

Notes:

- Since television and radio have such an impact on our values, do you feel the violence in the media (TV, movies) is partly responsible for some of society's ills?

- Is our society becoming too desensitized?

- Is TV guilty of sensationalism?

- Are TV talk shows too exploitive and too crude?

- Have you established a set of values or a belief system?
    If so, in what ways?

- Are your abilities limitless?

- Do you acknowledge your own limitations?

- Is there a universal sense of right and wrong?

140

Notes:

- Do you feel people are basically good or evil?

- Are people born that way, or is it learned?

- Can values be taught?

- Does religion play a role in any of this?

- Did you receive any religious training?

- How often do you go to church (or temple)?

- Do you read the Bible (or a prayer book)?

- What is your favorite scripture (or passage)?

- Do you believe in God?

- Describe your relationship with God

Notes:

- Tell me about the changes of pace you've seen in society

- Have you seen a change in your daily life – patterns, routines?

- Is traffic affecting the way we live?

- As a child, was ice delivered to your home?

- Was milk delivered to your door?

- Is it accurate to suggest that when you were growing up, people talked more to one another?

- Was there less fear of walking alone?

- When you were young, was there a strong sense of the neighborhood as a social community?

Notes:

- How have advances in technology changed us?

- Are things too fast now?

- Tell me about technology changes you've seen

      Describe what the cars looked like.

      Were there trolley cars?

      Airlines?

      Describe the telephone in your home.

      Did you go to the movies?

      Do you remember your family's first TV set?

      Can you describe it?

- Do you have a color TV

      VCR?

      CD Player?

      Fax machine?

      Personal computer?

- Any you <u>don't use?</u>

Notes:

- Are you comfortable with these things?

  Do you appreciate what they do?

- We've seen major world changes - the fall of
  Communism, our alliance with Russia, AIDS,
  urban riots ...

  What do you see for the future?

- Any thoughts on the next ten years as far as:

  Major world events?

  The economy?

  Will things get better or worse?

  How about technology? Any thoughts
  on what's to come?

  How our life-styles might change?

  Will our quality of life improve?

  Our standard of living?

  Improvements in race relations?

  Will things get worse?

Notes:

- Are you optimistic about the future?

    If not, why not?

- What have you experienced in your lifetime, that you hope will be spared from your grandchildren?

- What advice do you have for your grandchildren?

We're winding up this interview, and future generations of your family will watch and listen to this biography. What do you want to say to them? Look right into the camera and take as much time as you'd like.

Thanks, (Subject name) for a terrific story. You've been very patient with these questions, and you've created a wonderful legacy for your family.

Be sure your Subject remains seated until the Camera Operator fades out and says, "Cut" before removing the microphones

Chapter 13

YOUNGSTER VIDEO BIOGRAPHY

In addition to the adult video biography, we've included a script for youngsters.

Wouldn't it be wonderful to capture the essence of a child?

Imagine the youngster's descendents being able to actually see what his/her father (or mother, grandmother, grandfather) was like as a child.

This script is directed toward youngsters between the ages of six to thirteen. Of course, depending on the youngster, this age range can be expanded, but you will have to modify the script accordingly. There are no pre-interview forms because there is not the background information as required with an adult.

In most cases the Moderator will be a parent, but not necessarily. There are questions in the script which ask the child their opinion of mom and dad. It's important to assure the child that being candid and honest is very important. We don't want to embarrass the child, but we do want their true feelings to come through. Therefore, a close friend or neighbor might be a good substitute as the Moderator to avoid the parents or child being embarrassed.

Tailor the questions (and word choice) to fit the

age and circumstances of the youngster. Since there may be a wide separation in age, some questions will not be appropriate for all youngsters. Allow the youngster to pause, stammer; and go into tangents. Use the responses to delve deeper.

Remember to be warm and personal, to give eye-contact, and to use the youngster's first name throughout the questions.

YOUNGSTER SCRIPT DATA

1. Today's date
2. City and state of residence
3. Subject's full name
4. Subject's date of birth
5. Parent's names
6. Name of Moderator

YOUNGSTER'S SCRIPT

Today is _____ and we're in the home
of _____ presenting a video
biography of _____,
who was born on _____ making
him/her _____ years old.

We're just going to talk for awhile, (Subject's
name)_____. Please answer these
questions as honestly and as best you can.
Ignore the camera and talk to me. Say anything

you want, okay?

- Do you have a nickname?

- Who started calling you that?

- Do you like that nickname?

- What kind of job does your father have?

- What kind of work does your mother do?

- How do you feel about your parents?
    Your mother?
    Your dad?
- What's the best thing about your mom?

- Is there one thing about her you don't like?

- What's the best thing about your dad?

Is there one thing about him you don't like?

Do your parents treat you fairly?

Are they too strict?

Do you ever get punished?
>How?
>Do you deserve it?

Do you have a brother(s)?
>How many?
>His name(s)?
>How old is each?

Do you have a sister(s)?
>How many?
>Her name(s)?
>How old is each?

- Do you like having an older brother (sister)?

- Do you like having a younger brother (sister)?

- How do you feel about your brother(s) and sister(s)?

- Do you get along with them?

- Do they pick on you?

- Do you pick on them?

- Would you like a baby brother (baby sister)?
  Why?
- Tell me about your grandparents.

- Where do they live?

- Do you like to visit them?

- Tell me about your aunts and uncles.

- What are their names?

- Where do they live?

- Do you like to visit them?

- What kind of family trips have you gone on?

- Where did you go?

- Who went on the trip(s)?

- How often did you take trips?

- Have you been to Disneyland?

- What's your favorite ride?

- Any other amusement parks?

- Have you ever gone camping with you family?

- What has been your favorite vacation?

- Where's the farthest place you've traveled away from home?

- Have you ever gone to camp?

- Do you have a babysitter?

- Is it okay when your parents go out and leave you with a sitter?

- How late do you stay up?

- What do you think about before you fall asleep?

- Do you dream at night?

- What do you dream about?

- Describe your bedroom.

- What's your favorite thing in your room?

    Why?

- Do you share your bedroom?

- Do you mind having to share your bedroom?

- What's the most important thing you own?

- How much of an allowance do you get?

- Is it a fair amount?

- What do you spend your money on?

- Are you saving any money?

- What are you saving it for?

- Do you have chores to do around the house?

- Do you mind doing these things?

- Do you actually like helping out?

- Who is your best friend?

- Where does he (she) live?

- How did you two first meet?

- What do you like about that person?

- What do you dislike about him/her?

- Do you think you'll always be best friends?

- Do you and your best friend share secrets?

- Can you share one with me?

- Tell me about some of your other friends.

- Where do they live?

- How did you meet them?

- What do you do when you get together?

- Are there any kids who you really don't like?

  Why?

- Have you ever had a crush on anyone?

- Tell me about it.

- How did she (he) make you feel?

- Do you have a boyfriend (girlfriend)?

- How do you feel about him (her)?

- What do the two of you do together?

- What school do you go to?

- What grade are you in?

- What is your teacher's (s) name(s)?

- Do you like school?

- What do you like (or dislike) about it?

- How are your grades? Please be honest!

- Have you ever gotten in trouble at school?

    Tell me about it.

- Were you ever in a fight?

    What happened?

- What is your favorite school subject?

- Which subject do you dislike the most?

- Who is the best teacher you've ever had?

- What makes her (him) so special?

- Which teacher do you especially dislike?

    Why?

    What subject does he (she) teach?

- Do you have too much homework?

- How do you feel about that?

    Why?

- What would you rather be doing after school?

- Have you thought about college?

    Do you want to go?

    What do you want to study?

    Are you aware how difficult it is to get in?

    Are you willing to work hard for good

    grades?

- Which college would you like to attend?

- Have you ever experimented with drugs?

- Ever tried smoking?

- Ever tried beer or alcohol?

- Do you know any kids who have?

- Do you think these things are harmful?

- Any kids you know who have tried sex?

- Any kids you know who have tried sex?

- Do you think it's right?

- Does your mom or dad read to you?

- Did they read to you when you were younger?

- Do you like to read by yourself?

- What do you read?

- What is (was) favorite bedtime story?

- What makes (made) it so special?

- What is the best present you ever received?

- Why is it so special?

- What's your favorite toy at the present?

- What was your favorite when you were young?

- Do you play with toy guns (action figures, dolls)?

- Do you pretend when you play?

- Tell me what you pretend about.

- Do you ever daydream?

- What do you daydream about?

- Do you have an imaginary friend?

- What is that person like?

- If your friend could be any cartoon or action figure, which one would you pick?

- Tell me why.

- If you found a magic genie who would grant you three wishes, what would you wish for?

- Why is the sky blue?

- What color would you like it to be?

    Why?

- What's your favorite restaurant?

- What is your favorite food?

- What food(s) do you dislike the most?

- What is your favorite drink?

- What's your favorite TV show?

- Are there any TV shows you can't watch?

- Do you know why?

- Do you think that's fair?

- Do you like video games?

- What's your favorite?

- Which one don't you like?
  Why?

- What was the last movie you saw in a theatre?

- Did you like it?

- Do you watch movies on the VCR?

- Do you own any?

- What's your favorite video?

  Why?

- Are there some movies your parents won't let you see?

- Do you know why?

- Do you think that's fair?

- What kind of music do you like?

- What's your favorite song?

- Would you sing it for me now?

- What's your favorite holiday? (Suggest a few: Halloween, Christmas)

  Why?

- Are you into sports?

- Which is your favorite?

- Are you on any after-school teams?

- What hobbies or interests do you enjoy?

- Do you play a musical instrument?

  Which one(s)?

- Are you good at it?

- Could you play something now?

- Do you know how to use a computer?

- What do you use it for?

- What kind of indoor games do you like?

- What are you really good at doing?

- What is it you'd like to do better?

- Who are your heroes?

- Who do you want to be like? (Suggest a few: sports figures, actors, astronauts.)

- Do you have any pets?

- What kind?

- What are their names?

- Do you help take care of them?

- If you could have any animal for a pet, what would it be?

    Why?

- Are you involved with any clubs or after-school activities?

- Do you belong to the Cub Scouts (Boy Scouts, Girl Scouts)?

- What are you particularly good at doing?

- Is there anything you find hard to do?

    What?

- What is it that you really don't like to do? Why?

- What would you really like to do, but your parents won't let you?

- Do you ever do anything that's wrong?

- Tell me about it

- How does it make you feel afterward?

- Have you ever lied?

- How did it make you feel?

- Have you ever cheated at school?

  How did it make you feel?
  Did you get caught?

What happened?

- Did you ever steal anything?

- How did it make you feel?

- Do you ever get punished?

- What did you do?

- What did your parents (teacher) do?

- Was it fair?

- What should we do with bad people?

- Is it a good thing to have jails?

- How does it make you feel when you see a

homeless person on the street?

- What makes you get scared?

- When was the last time that happened?

- Do you believe in ghosts?

- What makes you get mad?

- When was the last time you got mad? Why?

- How do you feel when you're mad?

- Have you ever been ashamed about anything you've done?

- Tell me about it.

- Ever done anything to make you feel proud?

- Do you wish you were older?

- How old would you like to be? Why?

- Do your parents still treat you like you're a child?

- In what ways?

- How did you celebrate your last birthday?

- What kind of presents did you get?

- What was your last Halloween costume?

- Tell me about it.

- Did you get lots of candy?

- What's your favorite candy?

- Have you ever been sick with a disease?
    What was it? Measles, chicken pox?

- How did it make you feel?

- Did your parents help make you feel better?

- Ever been in the hospital? For what?

- What did the doctor do to help?

- Which do you hate going to the most:: the regular doctor or the dentist?

    Why?

- Do you like jokes?

- Could you tell me one?

- Who's the worst driver, your mom or your dad?   Tell me why.

- How far back can you remember?

- Tell me about your earliest memory

- Can you imagine what it would be like to be married?

- How do you picture it?

- Do you think you'll make a good parent?

- What kind of work do you want to do?

- Is it more important to be rich or to be happy? Why?

- What do you really like about yourself?

- Is there anything about yourself you wish you could change?

- Do you go to church (temple)?

- Do you like going, or do you go only because your parents want you to?

- Do you pray?

- Tell me about your prayers.

- What do you think happens after you die?

- Do you believe in God?

- Do you believe in heaven?

- Tell me about God.

- What kind of adult do you think you'll become?

- What kind of parent will you be?

- What do you think the world will be like when you have kids your age?

- Generally speaking, are you happy?

- Are you enjoying your life?

- Is there anything you wish could be different?

- Many years from now, your children will watch this when they're your age. What do you want to say to them?

Thank you, _____. You did a great job!

Create a Video Biography

Chapter 14

The Final Product

The final product should be an attractive, self-contained unit. One way to achieve this "look" is to use labels with your Subject's name and the date of the taping .

Avery ® makes blank labels for both the spine and face of VHS cassettes. These labels can be formatted on a personal computer and printed on any popular printer. There's no need to buy a computer label program. The company supplies an easy-to-read software guide. Placing labels on the front and spine of both the cassette and its sleeve will make for easy identification.

If your Subject or your Subject's family wants additional copies, there are two choices:

1. The Camera Operator may edit each copy separately from the original camera copy. This way, your Subject will have multiple second generation copies. This can be time consuming.

2. It may be worthwhile to have a professional tape duplicating house make your copies. They have superior technical equipment and will produce excellent copies.

Often, the Subject gives the original to the children. Whoever gets the video needs to care for and handle it properly. Some people have several copies made professionally and keep the master in a safe deposit box. After all, it's a legacy for the family.

If the person entrusted decides to keep the master tape in the home, the following procedures should be followed:

1. Store the cassette in a cool, dry, dust-free environment
2. Store the cassette upright – like a book on a shelf. Do not lay it flat
3. Avoid direct sunlight
4. Keep the cassette away from magnetic fields
5. Rewind the tape once a year
6. If storing for an extended period of time, wind the tape forward so there is an equal amount of tape on each spool

The accidental erasure of a tape can be avoided by breaking off the tab on the rear of the cassette.

The shelf life of today's tape is about fifteen years.

This means that if you want your taped biography to be handed down to future generations, you must make copies within that period. These copies should be professionally made in order to maintain the original quality.

Technology is moving rapidly toward media with almost indefinite shelf life, i.e., CD-ROMS, DVD, etc. For your tape treasures, consider copying your tape to one of these new media. It is strongly recommended you consider this option.

CHAPTER *15*

COMMON QUESTIONS

The authors have professionally taped hundreds of biographies. The script in this book has undergone many versions and changes. What you have in this script is the result of these hundreds of taping sessions.

These are our recommendations. We strongly urge you to follow them. This is not to say the script shouldn't be modified to suit individual circumstances. It should. However, we feel you'll be quite pleased with the results of following our outline.

The following questions have been asked of us in our professional tapings, and the answers may help you feel more comfortable.

Q. Why not share the questions with the Subject before the actual taping session?

A. Allowing your Subject to know the questions in advance robs the interview of its spontaneity. Other than a brief explanation of what to expect, there should be no advance disclosure. Your Subject must hear the questions for the first time on camera. We want to see the "wheels turn." Spontaneity reveals the Subject's true personality, and that's what you want handed down – not a canned rehearsal.

Example: the Subject is informed that he or she will be asked about their favorite TV show of all time. An answer is memorized and rattled off. The family is then robbed of seeing your Subject think and reflect. It's not only what is said, but how it's said that reflects an individuals persona. It's process over content. That's where the gems come from.

Q. Why go to your Subject's home with all of the equipment in tow, when it would be easier if the person came to you?

A. We have found that capturing the Subject on tape in their own environment gives more of a complete picture of who the person is. Whether in a family room, living room, or den – it's part of their essence. In the background of the shot and surrounding the person, the viewer will see various objects which reflect the individual's identity – objects on the coffee table, pillows by their side, paintings on the wall, etc.

Your Subject will be more comfortable and at ease when the taping session is conducted in the familiar environment of their own home. Putting the Subject at ease is a major element of a successful taping.

Finally, it's more convenient if your Subject wants an "enhancement option." Old photographs are at home, in an album or framed on display. The favorite activity or "hobby insert" (painting, gardening. etc.) is likely to be located within the person's home.

Q. If we're extending the effort of going to the Subject's house, why bring two folding chairs?

A.. Many people will tend to slouch if in a comfortable sofa or easy chair. Slouching is unflattering, particularly when the camera pulls back. People will sit up straighter and have better posture in a folding chair. This is the best of both worlds. Your Subject is at home and sitting up straight.

Q. Why should your Subject wear casual attire?

A. The video biography is not designed to be a stiff, formal portrait. While the Moderator could be somewhat formally dressed, your Subject should be seen as he or she usually is - casual and informal. Casual attire will help to create a more comfortable, relaxed mood.

Q. Does your Subject need makeup?

A. Generally not. If the subject is female, then powder and lipstick are in order. It's not necessary for the Subject to wear additional makeup. Older people may have spots and wrinkles, but these can be softened by diffusing the light and avoiding extreme close-ups. There's nothing wrong showing one's age. Allow the Subject to be who they are.

An exception may be if your Subject has a temporary blemish or sore. Using makeup to cover the spot will allow the person to feel more attractive and less self-conscious.

Q. Why should we minimize editing ?

A. Unless you're a pro, don't "over-edit." See the chapter, *Editing to Enhance.*

Subjects can't be expected to give flawless presentations. No one is looking for a perfect performance. People want to see what grandmother looked like, hear about her life, and what she had to say about things. It's okay for your Subject to flub, stammer, and even grope for the proper word. Editing should limited to the following circumstances:

1) Changing cassettes
2) Technical problems

3) Unexpected noises (airplane) or distractions

4) At the request of your Subject

5) Cuts to the "optional enhancement" insertions – (titles, old photographs, etc.).

Q. Why is the Moderator barely visible on camera?

A. This is the Subject's story, not the Moderator's. Reaction shots of the Moderator's responses are unnecessary and inappropriate. Shots showing your Subject and Moderator facing one another are unnecessary.

All that needs to be seen is your Subject speaking – sometimes zooming in for a tight shot, and sometimes pulling back to reveal the head shoulder of the Moderator. We see the back of the Moderator with your Subject which allows the viewer to get a feel for the sitting arrangement.

Q. Why do we discourage a married couple from doing one video biography?

A. The interview is of one's life story; not a couple's. In many cases, one spouse is more dominate. This can lead to the more submissive spouse being unnaturally quiet. So much time is spent on the aspects of one's early life, the other person may be a distraction. Significant time is spent discussing the spouse, (how they met, the courtship, etc.), so the flavor of the marriage is intact. The perspective should be from the Subject's point of view and their life story. We suggest making two biographies – not the couple's.

Good luck!

Appendix

We have provided an additional set of Profile Sheets since these are to be completed by the Subject. For your convenience, these sheets are perforated so they may be removed and copied for several interviews.

Subject Information Sheet

- Date of scheduled interview _____

- City where you currently live_____

- Your full name _____

- Your date of birth_____

- Your primary career

  _____

  _____

- Are you currently retired? _____

- Name of current spouse (if applicable)

  _____

- Number of years married to current spouse

  _____

- Name(s) of previous spouse(s) and number of years married (if applicable)

  _____

  _____

- List the name(s) of your children and grand-children (if applicable) and birth-dates

  _____

  _____

  _____

  _____

  _____

  _____

  _____

- With which spouse (if applicable)

  _____

  _____

  _____

Create a Video Biography

1. Education

   Did you attend high school?   Yes   No

   Did you attend college?   Yes   No

2. Talents/Skills/Abilities

   _____

   _____

   _____

   _____

   _____

3. Accomplishments/Achievements

   _____

   _____

   _____

   _____

4. Awards/Honors/Scholarships

   _____

   _____

   _____

5. Did you serve in the military?   Yes   No

    a. Which Branch _____

    b.When did you serve? _____

    c. Were you overseas?   _____

    Where?

_____

_____

6. Additional careers/Jobs

_____

_____

_____

7. Places/Countries you've traveled

_____

_____

8. Hobbies/Interests

_____

_____

_____

9. Stories/Anecdotes_____

_____

_____

_____

10. Any other specific occurrence, experience, or event you wish to be included?

_____

_____

_____

_____

Be sure to avoid memorizing any "canned" responses from the profile sheets. We want to see the "wheels" turning. More important than what you say is how you say it – in your mannerisms, your style. Your personality will shine through.